Around the World

FASHION

Sketchbook

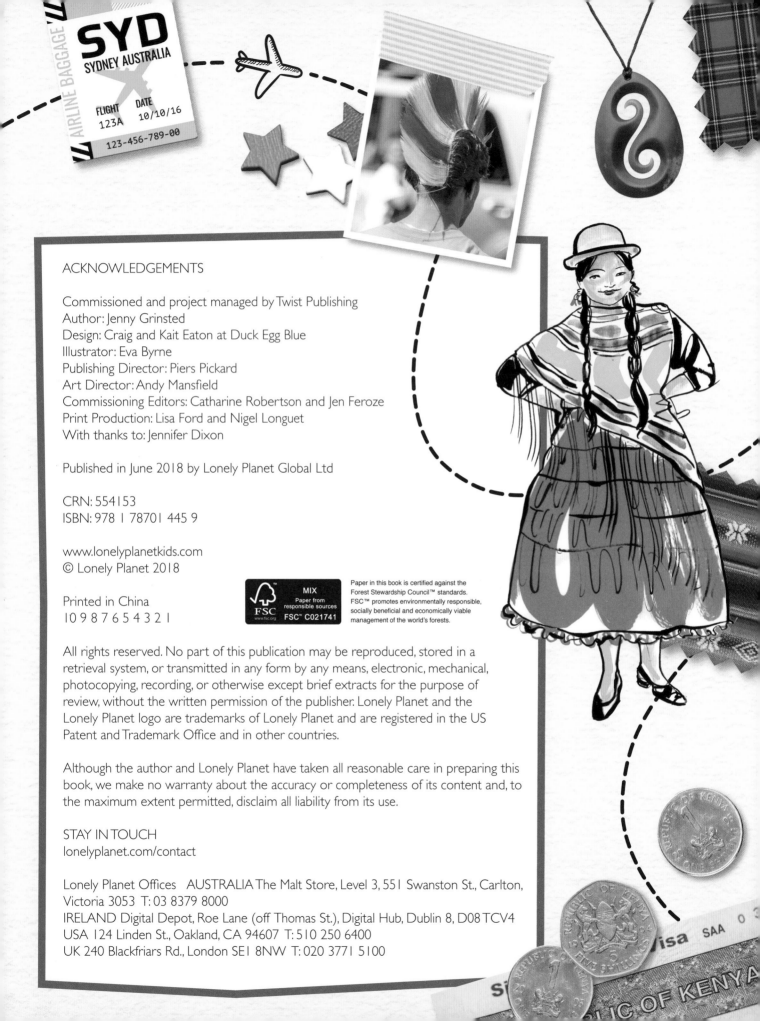

ACKNOWLEDGEMENTS

Commissioned and project managed by Twist Publishing
Author: Jenny Grinsted
Design: Craig and Kait Eaton at Duck Egg Blue
Illustrator: Eva Byrne
Publishing Director: Piers Pickard
Art Director: Andy Mansfield
Commissioning Editors: Catharine Robertson and Jen Feroze
Print Production: Lisa Ford and Nigel Longuet
With thanks to: Jennifer Dixon

Published in June 2018 by Lonely Planet Global Ltd

CRN: 554153
ISBN: 978 1 78701 445 9

www.lonelyplanetkids.com
© Lonely Planet 2018

Printed in China
10 9 8 7 6 5 4 3 2 1

MIX
Paper from
responsible sources
FSC™ C021741
www.fsc.org

Paper in this book is certified against the Forest Stewardship Council™ standards. FSC™ promotes environmentally responsible, socially beneficial and economically viable management of the world's forests.

STAY IN TOUCH
lonelyplanet.com/contact

Lonely Planet Offices   AUSTRALIA The Malt Store, Level 3, 551 Swanston St., Carlton, Victoria 3053 T: 03 8379 8000
IRELAND Digital Depot, Roe Lane (off Thomas St.), Digital Hub, Dublin 8, D08 TCV4
USA 124 Linden St., Oakland, CA 94607 T: 510 250 6400
UK 240 Blackfriars Rd., London SE1 8NW T: 020 3771 5100

Around the World
FASHION
Sketchbook

Written by
Jenny Grinsted

Illustrated by
Eva Byrne

Contents

Your style journey!

Welcome to your worldwide fashion adventure! No matter where you live or what you wear, we all use clothes to tell the world who we are, for practical purposes, and to mark special occasions. Get ready to doodle, design, and sketch your way from New York City to Australia — and everywhere else along the way!

Don't forget to pack some pencils for sketching along the way!

Europe
(p30)

Asia
(p54)

Africa
(p42)

Australia and Southeast Asia
(p66)

Turn the page to start your journey.

North America

From modern urban styles to traditional Native American clothes and from tropical to snowy outfits, the fashion of North America is as varied as its peoples and weather.

BOARDING PASS
AMERICAN AIRWAYS

NAME/SURNAME		DATE	TIME
K. BROWN		**10 DEC**	**0845**
FROM		GATE	SEAT
HAWAII ISLANDS		**A10**	**08B**
DESTINATION	FLIGHT		
NAVAJO NATION (ARIZONA)	**RQEVR435**		

ECONOMY

NAME	K. BROWN	
FROM	HAWAII ISLANDS	
TO	NAVAJO NATION (ARI)	
DATE	10 DEC	TIME 0845
GATE	A10	SEAT 08B
FLIGHT	RQEVR435	

123654

Navajo Nation, US
(p10)
Design turquoise jewelry and explore Navajo traditions.

Hawaii, US
(p8)
Discover styles born from a unique mix of cultures.

Nunavut, Canada
(p16)
Dressing for extremes. Brrrrr!

FORT ST JOHN BC
PROPLINERS
CANADA
859912

Rhode Island, US
(p14)
Celebrate Independence Day in red, white, and blue.

New York City, US
(p12)
Street style and hip-hop!

BAGGAGE (STRAP) TAG
No. Checked Pcs.   Total Weight
SEE REVERSE SIDE
NYC
New York City · USA
B- 54-88-11

Hawaii, US

Aloha! Welcome to sunny, tropical Hawaii – and to some unique styles formed by the mixing of different cultures. Polynesian, Chinese, Portuguese, Japanese, and many other settlers have influenced this island paradise's fashion!

Full pāʻū (say pah-oo) skirts

Aloha (or Hawaiian) shirts developed from Japanese fabrics.

Give this pāʻū skirt and aloha shirt bright, Hawaiian-inspired designs.

Lei garlands (made from flowers, shells, leaves, nuts, or feathers)

Ti-leaf skirt

Styling note:

Pā'ū and ti-leaf skirts are only worn on special occasions, but aloha shirts are worn every day!

Fabulously bright designs often feature tropical plants.

Navajo Nation, US

The style of the Native American Navajo (say *nava*-ho) people includes dramatic turquoise jewelry and woven dresses made from blanket-like materials.

Turquoise has spiritual significance in Navajo culture.

Jewelry is worn by all ages!

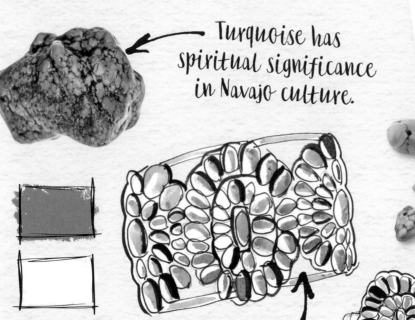

The turquoise is set in silver.

Design your own range of stunning turquoise and silver jewelry.

Biil dress made from two woven panels stitched together

This type of necklace is called a "squash blossom" necklace.

Traditional leggings

Woven Navajo designs are intricate and geometric.

Styling note:

Today, biil dresses are not worn every day, but may be worn at graduation ceremonies.

Navajo Art USA **22**
A Museum of the American Indian

vintage stamp showing a Navajo rug

New York City, US

Street fashion in New York City is inspired by hip-hop. This famous music and dance style started in the Bronx area of New York in the 1970s. Today, many hip-hop stars have created their own clothing ranges.

Baseball cap

Loose jeans, pants, or shorts

Sneakers

Baggy T-shirt

Clothes often include logos (small symbols) to tell you who designed them.

Design a logo for your own range of hip-hop-inspired clothes.

Street art is an important part of hip-hop culture.

Loose clothes are easy to break-dance in.

Look at the hundreds of styles in this New York sneaker store!

Customize this sneaker using whatever colors and designs you want.

Rhode Island, US

Every year on July 4, Americans remember the 1776 signing of the Declaration of Independence. One of the most famous celebrations is in Bristol, Rhode Island, where they have celebrated every year since 1785!

Independence Day outfits are inspired by the US flag.

The Bristol parade includes bands and drummers.

Stars and stripes

Tuesday, July 4

10:30 a.m. Watch Independence Day parade

5 p.m. BBQ

9 p.m. Fireworks!

Red, white, and blue

Americans create all kinds of unique Independence Day outfits and styles!

Decorate these children's outfits in red, white, and blue for an Independence Day celebration.

Nunavut, Canada

The climate in Nunavut, northern Canada, is incredibly harsh – winter lasts for eight months of the year, and temperatures can drop to -120°F (about -50°C)! Combining warmth with style and tradition is essential for the Inuit people who live there.

Animal skins

Thick woolen cloth

Modern man-made waterproof fabrics

Mittens, a cosy coat, and a hat or hood are essential!

Styling note:

Inuit fashion mixes and matches traditional and modern materials.

The English words "anorak" and "parka" (both meaning "coat") come from the Inuits' Inuktitut language.

Canada 17

Inuit – Spirits Les Inuits – Le surnaturel

Stamp with design by a famous Inuit artist called Kenojuak Ashevak.

Inner stocking

+

Boot

+

Over-slipper

=

Traditional multilayered boots called kamiks

Warm but not very waterproof!

The boots are made from caribou hide or sealskin.

Waterproof but not so warm!

Warm doesn't have to be boring!
Design your own stylish cold-weather outfit here.

South and Central America

Fashion in South and Central America is a unique blend of African, European, and <u>indigenous</u> influences, creating vibrantly colored and patterned clothing.

Indigenous means the people who lived in South America before Europeans and Africans arrived.

Mexico
p20
Celebrate the skeletal Day Of the Dead!

Bolivia
p24
Explore the Aymará people's unique fashion.

ARGENTINA
BUENOS AIR
FLIGHT: 84-44-43

Argentina
p28
Discover Argentine cowboy style.

WELCOME TO JAMAICA

Jamaica
(p22)

Twirl in a
red-and-white
quadrille dress!

Brazil
(p26)

Design a fabulous
feathered headdress for
a Carnaval performer.

Mexico

Called Día de los Muertos in Spanish!

The vibrant and colorful <u>Day of the Dead</u> is one of the most important holidays in Mexico. Indigenous beliefs say that the spirits of the dead can return to their homes at this time of year.

Bright colors make the festival a celebration of those who have died.

People paint their faces to look like skulls.

Paint this model's face, ready for a Day of the Dead-inspired fashion show.

20

Indigenous Mexican style also includes intricately embroidered tunics called huipiles.

Embroidery pattern made from lots of tiny stitches

Different communities have different designs.

Create your own embroidered design for a huipil.

Jamaica

Did you know that in Jamaica there's a dress named after a dance? *Quadrille* dresses are named after a Caribbean dance style that combines European and African influences.

Red, white, and blue plaid

Cool, light materials such as calico

Styling note:

Today, quadrille dresses are mainly worn for dance performances.

Straw hat

Head wrap called a bandana

The blouse is trimmed with plaid fabric.

Rows of white lace decorate the skirt.

Sometimes quadrille dresses are black, green, and gold to match the Jamaican flag!

How to draw a quadrille dress!

Step 1
Draw the outline of the body.

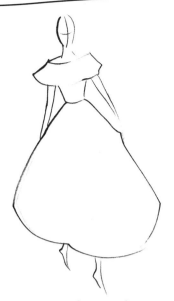

Step 2
Add the outlines of the dress and arms.

Step 3
Fill in detail on the dress. Add a head wrap.

Step 4
Add red, white, and blue to complete the dress.

Now try drawing your own quadrille dress!

Bolivia

The fashion of the indigenous Aymará women of Bolivia is colorful and distinctive, but also practical for the fierce sunlight and extreme temperatures of high-altitude living.

Styling note:

Bowler hats were introduced to Bolivia by Europeans. These days, the fashion has almost died out in Europe and North America but is still super-popular in Bolivia!

Vibrant colors

Bowler hat

Shawl

Sweater

Pleated skirt

Aguayo (piece of cloth used as a sling)

Two braids

Horizontal patterns

Petticoats underneath

24

Fabrics are woven from alpaca, llama, or vicuña wool.

Use bright colors to complete this Bolivian-style fabric pattern.

Customize your own bowler hat with colors and accessories!

Brazil

Carnaval is a spring festival celebrated all over Brazil. The most famous celebrations are in Rio de Janeiro, where different <u>samba</u> schools parade through the Sambódromo stadium while drumming, dancing, singing, and wearing incredible costumes.

Samba is a type of dance.

Feathered headdresses can be up to 5 feet (1.5 meters) tall.

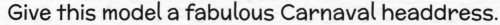

Give this model a fabulous Carnaval headdress.

The Sambódromo can seat 90,000 people!

Some dancers, called baianas, twirl in hooped skirts.

Saturday, Feb. 25

2 p.m. Pick up costume.

Don't forget, the word in Portuguese is fantasia.

Sunday, Feb. 26

9 p.m. Sambódromo parade!

Thousands of sequins and jewels make the costumes dazzle.

Add a sequin design to this cuff bracelet!

Try these colors.

27

Argentina

Argentine cowboys, or gauchos, roam the country's vast grasslands. Their clothes are tough and practical, designed for horseback riding, herding cattle and sheep, and surviving in remote locations.

Styling note:

For fiestas (festivals) gauchos wear full traditional costume. Everyday wear is usually a mix of traditional and modern elements.

Traditional beret or broad-brimmed sombrero hat

Poncho

Loose pants, called bombachas

A gaucho's knife is called a facón.

Wide leather and metal belt

Gaucho lasso

Tough leather boots with spurs

Ponchos often feature geometric designs.

Color this geometric fabric pattern.

For fiestas the horses dress up, too!

Give this horse a decorative bridle for a fiesta.

Europe

European fashion is both old and new, mixing centuries-old traditions with some of the most cutting-edge styling in the world.

AF 4155671

À To **PAR**

Paris (France)

VOL/Flight

AF 4-15-56-

BAGGAGE STRAP TA

Scotland
(p34)

Sketch your own clan tartan.

France
(p38)

Check out a catwalk show in the fashion capital of the world.

Spain
(p40)

Olé! visit a flamenco club and discover some fabulous dancewear.

Norway
(p32)
Discover a fantastic
bridal crown.

Germany
(p36)
Get dressed up for one of
Europe's biggest parties!

Norway

Elaborate, hand-made *bunad* clothes are worn in Norway on special occasions. Different regions have their own unique designs, and outfits can cost thousands of dollars!

women's outfits usually include a matching purse.

In a traditional Norwegian wedding, the bride wears a bunad plus a fabulous crown.

Cotton blouse

woolen skirt

Decorate this bunad purse, ready for a special occasion!

Elaborate gold or silver jewelry

Detailed embroidery

Color this embroidery design.

Try using these colors.

Scotland

Tartan is particularly associated with Scotland. Known as plaid in the US, it is a pattern of crisscrossed horizontal and vertical bands in multiple colors. Traditionally, each family, or clan, has its own unique tartan with its own name.

Black Watch tartan

Royal Stewart tartan

Campbell tartan

Bagpipes are a traditional Scottish instrument.

Kilt

Sporran (a bag worn over the kilt)

A kilt pin holds the kilt together.

A sgian dubh (pronounced skee-an doo) is a small dagger kept in the sock.

Knee-length socks

34

The first mention of tartan in Scotland was as long ago as 1538!

Tartan patterns inspire fashion designers around the world.

Women sometimes wear a tartan sash over a ballgown.

Ask an adult to help you look up your family tartan online, or design one yourself!

My surname . . . .

My family tartan design

My fashion design using my family tartan

(It could be a kilt, skirt, sash, or even an accessory such as a bag!)

Germany

Go to Munich in October, and you'll see people everywhere wearing dresses with full skirts called *dirndl* and leather shorts called *lederhosen* as they celebrate Oktoberfest, one of Europe's biggest parties.

Styling note:

Leather was originally used for pants because it is incredibly hard-wearing!

Suspenders hold up the lederhosen.

Silver chains, called charivari, are decorated with coins, charms, gems, and animal teeth.

Hang things from this chain to design your own charivari.

Tight-laced bodice

If the knot is tied on the right side, it means the wearer is married or has a partner!

Apron in contrasting color

Customize this dirndl with your favorite colors and patterns!

France

Many people think Paris, the capital of France, is also the capital of world fashion! French fashion designers' cutting-edge clothes create trends around the world, particularly in Europe and North America.

Fabulous gowns for special occasions

Stylish everyday wear

Designers use luxurious fabrics, such as cashmere, lace, and velvet.

Ballgown design master class

Step 1
Draw the outline of the model's body.

Step 2
Add the shape of the dress.

Step 3
Fill in the detail of the dress and hairstyle.

Step 4
Add color!

French designer Coco Chanel (1883-1971) forever changed the way we dress by making clothes less formal and easier to wear.

Coco Chanel introduced lots of styles we take for granted!

Pajamas for girls and women

Little black dresses

Bobbed hair

Now draw your own Parisian-style ballgown!

Spain

The famous flamenco dancers of southern Spain wear distinctive dresses with ruffled skirts. The dancers' complex, graceful hand movements are used to express their feelings.

Dancers sometimes use accessories such as fringed shawls, fans, and castanets.

Many dresses are decorated with polka dots.

The full skirt swishes as the dancer moves.

Doodle a lacy pattern on this flamenco fan.

A fitted bodice shows off the dancer's proud posture.

Design a flamenco-inspired dress to dance in.

The dancer stamps her high-heeled shoes to create a rhythm.

Thursday, July 22

10:30 p.m. Flamenco performance at La Carbonería, Seville

Don't forget!!!!

Africa

African fashion changes from country to country but is usually bright and bold, featuring vibrant patterns and dramatic jewelry.

Morocco
(p44)

Find out about jewelry said to ward off evil.

Ghana
(p46)

Design your own ankara cloth.

REPUBLIC OF GHANA
ACCRA
KOTOKA INTERNATIONAL AIRPORT
08 MARCH 2017

Angola
(p50)

Head to a Mumuhuila hairdresser!

Kenya
(p48)

Learn the language of beads with the Maasai communities of Kenya.

Namibia
(p52)

Discover the Herero women's fabulous full-length dresses.

Morocco

Silver headdress

Moroccan Berber jewelry is striking, symbolic, and practical all at the same time. Some designs (called amulets) are said to protect against ill fortune, and the jewelry is also a way to carry your wealth around with you!

Silver is inlaid with other precious materials such as amber and jade.

A hand-shaped amulet is said to protect the wearer from jealousy or evil.

Design your own amulet.
What would it protect you from?

My amulet would protect me from

44

Moroccan men and women both wear djellaba robes, with a multipurpose pointed hood that protects against sun, sand, cold, rain, or snow.

woolen djellabas are often woven with striped designs.

Add your own striped design to this djellaba.

45

Ghana

Brightly dyed and wonderfully patterned cotton fabrics, usually called ankara or <u>Dutch</u> wax prints, are central to style in West African countries such as Ghana. There are thousands of different designs!

Dutch traders introduced the ankara printing technique (based on Indonesian batik fabric) to West Africa.

People choose designs that reflect their personal style.

How to create an ankara print

1. Paint a pattern onto cotton using resin (a sort of varnish).
2. Dye the fabric. The dye will only stain the parts of the fabric not covered with resin.
3. When the fabric is dry, remove the resin. The fabric will now be patterned!
4. Repeat as many times as you want to create more and more complex patterns!

Cracked wax patterning

Ankara prints influence fashion around the world!

Designs are inspired by everything from traditional art to West African daily life to pop music.

Design your own wax print and write down what inspired it!

My wax print design was inspired by ....

Kenya

Women often wear wide disk necklaces.

Beads talk in the Maasai communities of Kenya and Tanzania! Different colors represent different parts of Maasai life, and the color combinations in Maasai jewelry are not just a fashion statement but also a statement about who the wearer is and what's important to them.

| the land | the people | bravery | purity | the sun | friendship | the sky |

Use the meaning of colors in Maasai culture to design a bead pattern.

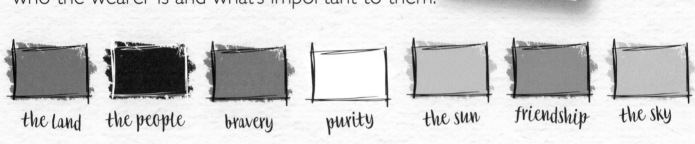

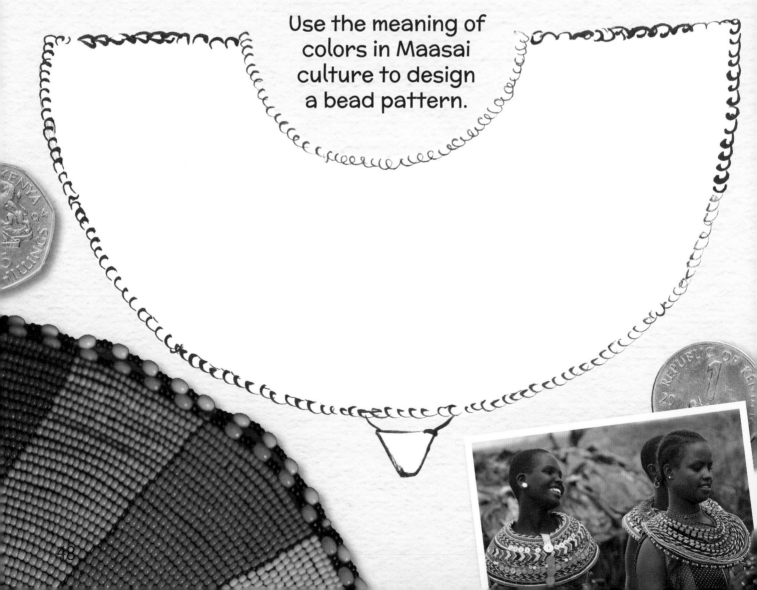

Both men and women wear bead jewelry.

Beaded headbands

Cloak called a shuka (usually red)

Give this girl a bright, beaded necklace and headband inspired by Maasai style.

Angola

Short, long, curly, straight, loose, braided – all over the world people use hairstyles to express their identities. In Angola, Mumuhuila women and girls sculpt their hair into thick locks called *nontombi* and decorate them with stunning accessories.

Styling note:

If you have only three nontombi, it means someone in your family has died.

Women usually wear four or six nontombi.

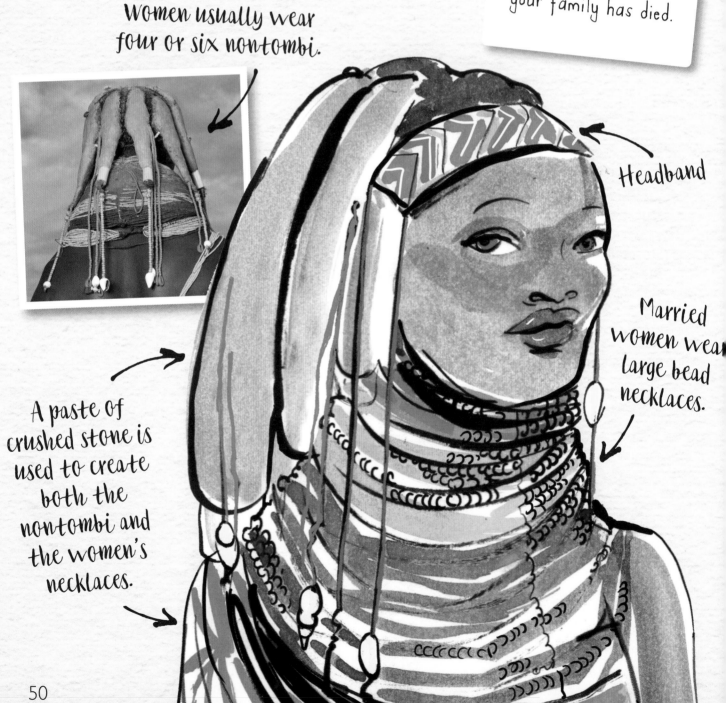

Headband

Married women wear large bead necklaces.

A paste of crushed stone is used to create both the nontombi and the women's necklaces.

Accessories such as shells and beads are added.

Diamond and arrow designs are popular.

Give this girl four different hairstyles.
How do they change how she looks?

They could be Mumuhuila styles, styles from where you live, or styles from another country in this book!

Namibia

Long, full dresses were worn in Europe in the late 1800s and early 1900s. In Europe today, they are worn only on special occasions – but the fashion survives in Namibia! There, it has developed into a dramatic and colorful style worn by women of the Herero communities.

Puffed sleeves

Long, full skirt

Tight bodice

Wide hat

Patchwork is part of Herero style.

Bring this patchwork pattern to life with color.

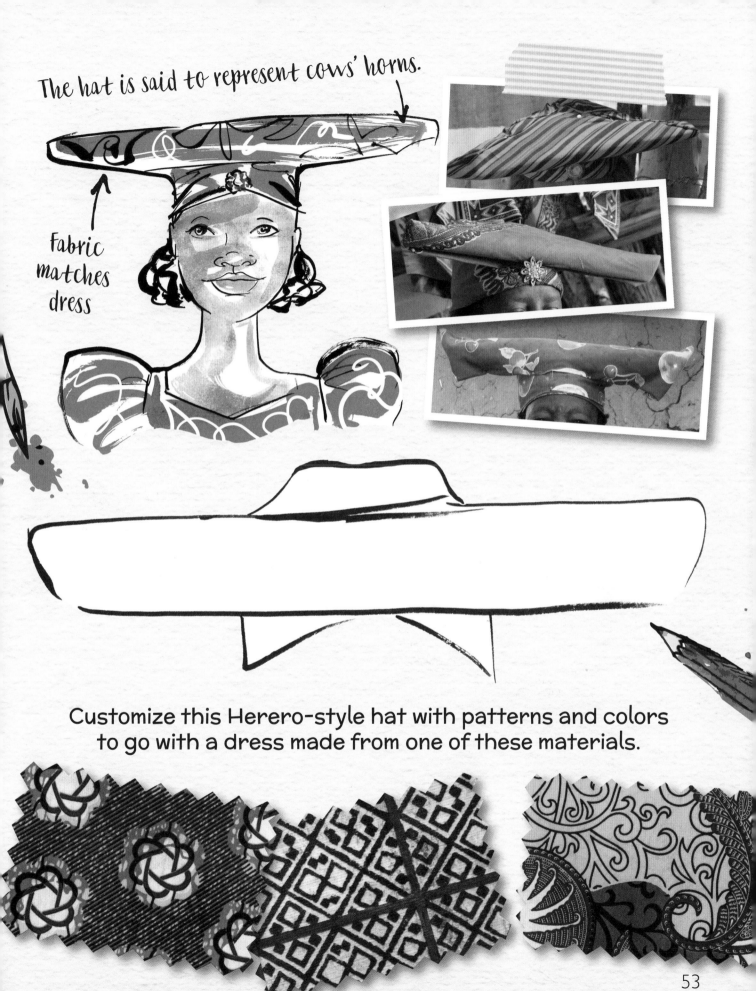

The hat is said to represent cows' horns.

Fabric matches dress

Customize this Herero-style hat with patterns and colors to go with a dress made from one of these materials.

Asia

Some of the world's most famous clothes come from Asia. Japanese kimonos, Indian saris, and Chinese *qipao* dresses are known around the world as graceful and stylish.

Mongolia
p60
Find out which clothes double as a tent!

Pakistan
p56
Customize a range of jeweled khussa slippers.

India
p58
Style up a sari!

China
p62
Explore what colors mean in Chinese culture.

Japan
p64
Discover elegant and elaborate formal kimonos.

Pakistan

Elaborate *khussa* slippers (also known as *mojari* or *jutti*) are worn in both Pakistan and India. The flat shoes are both practical and beautiful and are still handmade in Pakistani cities such as Lahore.

In the 1600s, emperors wore khussa slippers decorated with real gems and actual gold and silver thread!

Leather

Glue helps to hold the upper and lower parts together.

Lots of embroidery

Hand stitching

Metallic threads, tassels, jewels, and mirrors may all be incorporated into the design.

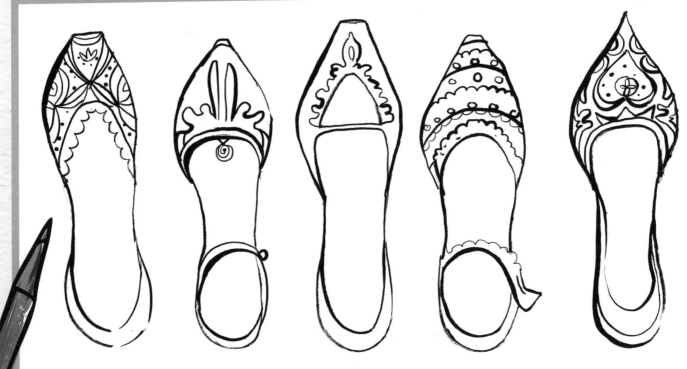

Add color to this row of slippers...

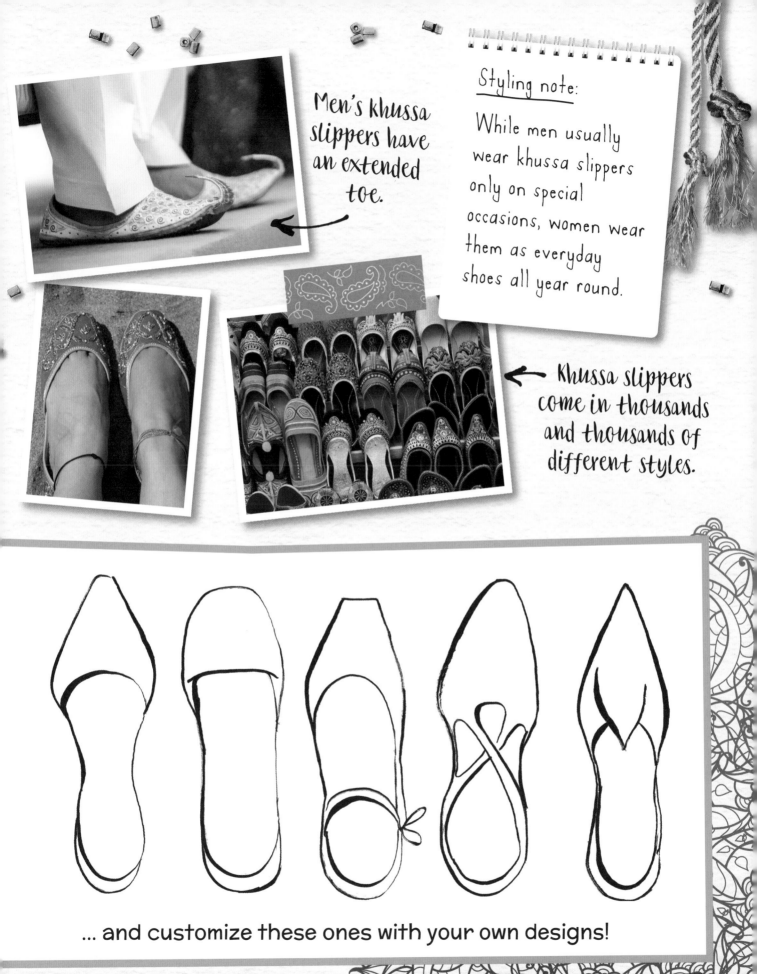

Men's khussa slippers have an extended toe.

While men usually wear khussa slippers only on special occasions, women wear them as everyday shoes all year round.

Khussa slippers come in thousands and thousands of different styles.

... and customize these ones with your own designs!

India

From high fashion to practical everyday wear, saris are everywhere in India! A sari is a long strip of fabric, usually wrapped around the waist and elegantly draped over one shoulder.

Styling note:

Loose clothes are practical and comfortable in a hot climate. India can be as hot as 120°F (around 50°C)!

There are lots of different ways to drape a sari.

Color these popular sari patterns.

A blouse is usually worn underneath a sari.

58

Top fashion designers create incredible saris with expensive fabrics and intricate patterns.

Everyday saris have simpler designs and use cheaper fabrics.

Use your favorite pattern to decorate this sari.

Mongolia

Mongolian *deels* are much more than just a nice outfit. They're designed for living on the country's huge open grasslands (called steppes) and surviving temperature extremes.

Styling note:

The loose wrap design means a deel can also be used as a blanket, or a sort of mini-tent for privacy when traveling the steppes.

Fur-lined hood or fur hat

High collar

Fastens at right shoulder with buttons

Buttons may be stones, silver, or intricate knots.

Long sleeves to protect hands from cold

Belt or sash

Summer deels are also silk but not padded.

Brightly colored silk lined with thick cotton padding or fur

Warm felt boots

Everyday deels may be gray or brown.

For special occasions, elaborate designs are paired with incredible headdresses.

Customize this deel with color, pattern, and a button design.

China

Colors mean different things in different cultures. In China, the colors used in clothes are influenced by the ancient Theory of the Five Elements. The Five Elements are water, fire, wood, metal, and earth, and each is associated with a different color.

Styling note:

White and black combine in this yin-and-yang design. It symbolizes balance or unity.

Green and blue are not always distinguished in Chinese. The character qing can mean either!

青
qing

Color	Element	Season	Symbolizes
Black	Water	Winter	Seriousness, formality
Red	Fire	Summer	Good fortune and joy
Green or blue	Wood	Spring	Health, new life, healing
White	Metal	Fall	Brightness, purity, sadness
Yellow	Earth	Change of seasons	Heroism, freedom, good luck

Black may be used for everyday work clothes.

Wedding clothes are traditionally red.

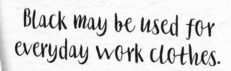

Color and decorate these clothes using the Theory of the Five Elements for inspiration.

A qipao dress

A zhongshan suit

Red and yellow are a classic combination for a qipao dress!

A dragon robe fit for an emperor

Japan

In Japan, kimonos are usually worn on formal occasions, such as during the tea ceremony. Both men and women wear kimonos, although the styling is slightly different.

Wrap the left side of the kimono over the right.

The kimono is held in place with a wide sash called an obi.

In the tea ceremony, serving tea turns into a form of art.

The sash can be tied in different ways.

Design a floral pattern for a kimono.

kimonos are often paired with elaborate hair accessories.

Decorate this girl's hair with Japanese-inspired accessories.

Thailand
(p68)

Learn how to draw
a Thai kŏhn dancer.

Indonesia
(p70)

You're invited to an
Indonesian wedding!

Australia and Southeast Asia

The region of Australia and Southeast Asia is a
patchwork of islands and peoples, and its fashion is
patchwork, too. From relaxed beachwear to ancient
and elaborate dance costumes, this is an area where
anything goes!

AIRLINE BAGGAGE

SYD
SYDNEY AUSTRALIA

FLIGHT   DATE
123A   10/10

Papua New Guinea
(p72)

Explore an island of amazingly varied cultures and styles!

Australia
(p74)

Surf's up! Design some stylish beachwear.

New Zealand
(p76)

Discover jade pendants and Maori culture.

Thailand

Kŏhn is a Thai art form that combines dance and drama. Performances are based on the *Ramakian*, an epic story of humans, gods, monkeys, and demons. Masks and costumes tell the audience what part each dancer is playing.

Richly patterned silk fabrics

Tall headdresses

Elaborate jewelry

women do not usually wear masks.

Learn how to draw a kŏhn dancer!

Step 1
Draw the outline of the dancer's body.

Step 2
Sketch the outline of the clothes.

Step 3
Fill in the detail of the clothes and headdress.

Step 4
Add color and a mask!

Thursday, October 12

7:30 p.m. Kŏhn performance at Sala Chalermkrung, Bangkok

Buy and read a copy of the Ramakian first!

The dancers don't speak, but the way they move tells the story.

Monkey mask

Now try drawing a kŏhn dancer yourself!

Indonesia

You're invited to an Indonesian wedding — along with hundreds, or even thousands, of other guests! Indonesian weddings are some of the biggest and most spectacular in the world, and absolutely everyone is invited to help the happy couple celebrate.

Batik fabric

Different but complementary outfits for the bride and groom

Intricate headdresses

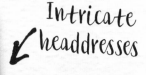

Styling note:

Colors, patterns, and styles are influenced by the couple's family background.

Color this batik pattern.

Some brides have their hands painted with henna patterns.

Create a henna pattern on this bride's hand.

Papua New Guinea

Everyone loves to dress up for a party, and people in Papua New Guinea are no different. When the island's hundreds of different cultures come together to celebrate at the Mount Hagen and Goroka Shows, the result is an explosion of color, style, and tradition.

Over 800 different languages are spoken in Papua New Guinea!

Face and body painting

Feathered headdresses

Elaborate necklaces often feature shells.

Get this boy ready for a party by painting his face!

Bilum bag

Bilum bags
are woven
from string.

Styling note:

Bilum bags are
for everyday use
as well as for
festive occasions.

There are
hundreds of
different
bilum designs!

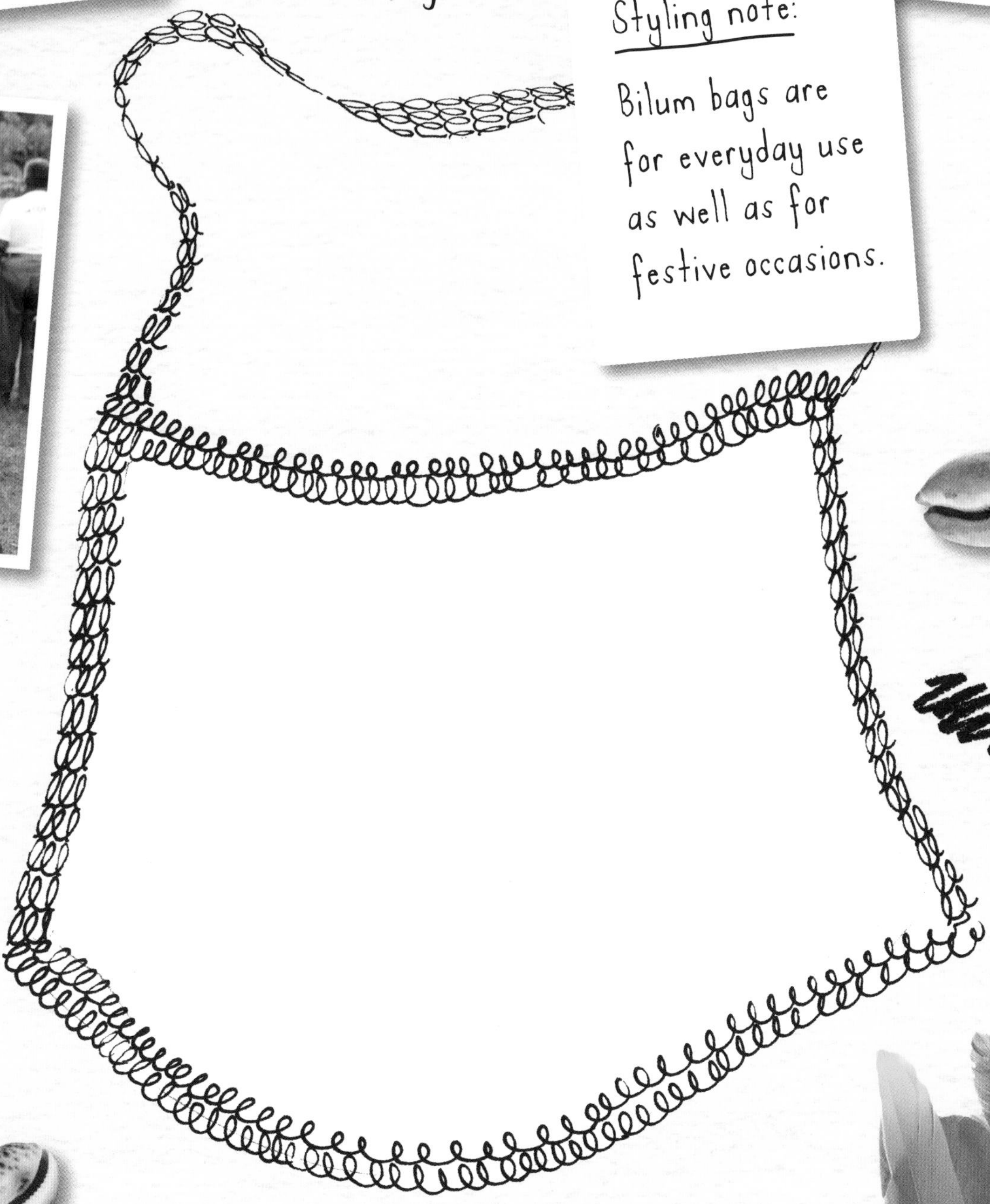

Doodle a pattern on this bilum bag.

Australia

Most Australians live close to the coast, so Australian fashion is influenced by beachwear and surfing style. Relaxed T-shirts, swimwear, and flip-flops are stylish and practical for long, sunny days on the sand.

Light, loose fabrics such as cotton

Swimsuits are often made from quick-drying synthetic fabrics.

Wetsuit to keep warm in the water

Give this T-shirt a surf-inspired design.

Flip-flops with colorful designs printed on them

Decorate this pair of flip-flops with colorful patterns.

Fiberglass surfboards

Surfing was probably invented by the ancient Polynesians.

Don't forget sunscreen and sunglasses!

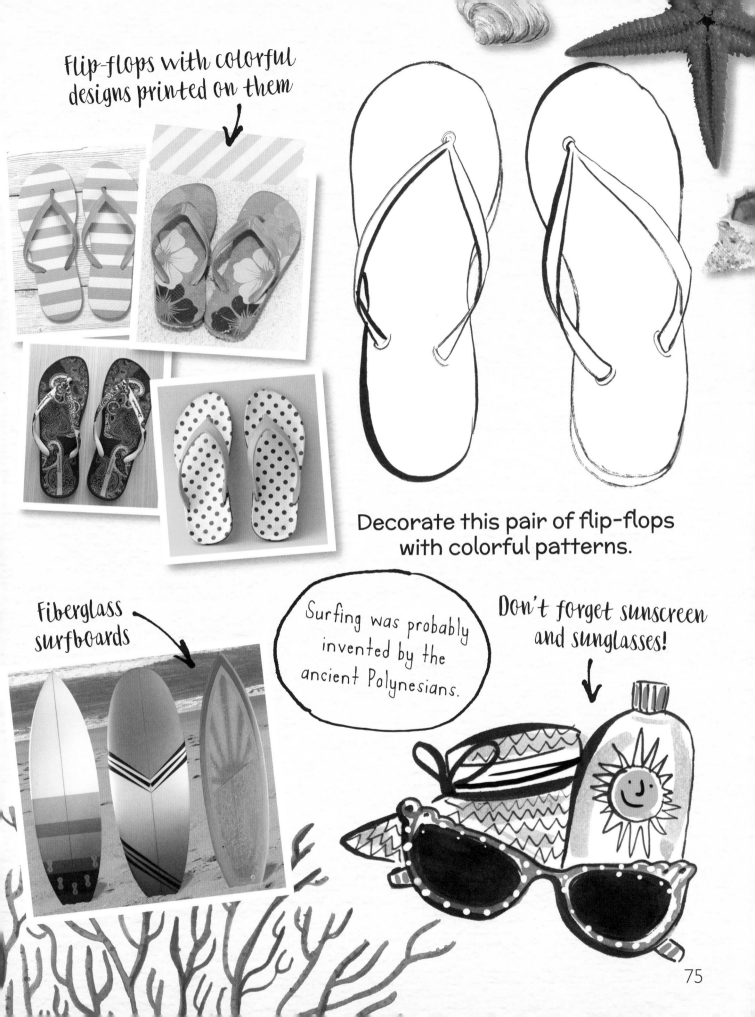

75

New Zealand

Dance is at the center of New Zealand's indigenous Maori culture, and feathered cloaks, flax skirts, and greenstone pendants are often worn when performing dances such as the warlike *haka* and graceful *poi*.

Poi ball

Poi dance

Cloaks are decorated with feathers. →

Flax skirt

Haka dance

Finish this feathered cloak.

Styling note:

Greenstone (a type of jade) is carved into many different designs, including the traditional heitiki symbol.

The fishhook is another traditional Maori design.

Cool vintage stamp showing a heitiki design

The ancestors of today's Maori people are thought to have arrived in New Zealand about 1,000 years ago.

Design a greenstone pendant to hang from this necklace.

Sketching pages

Use these pages to sketch your own fashion ideas inspired by this book!